Inquire Within

Questions For The Inspired Mind

Reviews

Inquire Within invites readers to cultivate the art of turning ordinary moments into extraordinary awareness by asking questions: essential questions, painful questions, respectful questions, loving questions. We inquire within not to receive illuminating answers, but to learn to love the practice of asking and living a conscious life. Like a stream meandering along a mountain path, the questions Pamela Wright ask tenderly flow over the sharp edges of being human and pool into deep, tranquil waters of reflection and appreciation for the grand mystery of the human experience.

Julie Clayton, New Consciousness Review

I have always savored Pam's incredibly flavorful cooking, but the richness of her food for thought has truly moved me. What a lovely gift for my closest female friends and associates.

Ann Louise Gittleman, Ph.D., CNS, New York Times bestselling author of 30 books on health and healing

***

A beautifully written and wise book that reawakens the deep, instinctual urge to explore and grow by asking questions in the artfully, potent way Pamela presents through stories. We once knew the mentoring power of questions as naturally open and curious children wanting to learn. Inquire Within takes this power to a whole new level of possibility in regard to profound discovery, essential inner growth, authenticity, deep insight, and heart-full connection with self and others.

Jeffrey Douglass, author, Living from Your Soul

Inquire Within

Questions For The
Inspired Mind

Pamela Wright

One Spirit Press
Portland, Oregon

ISBN: 978-1-893075-91-7
Library of Congress Control Number: 2012939894

Cover Design and Original Art Ethan Firpo
Book Design Spirit Press, LLC

One Spirit Press
www.onespiritpress.com
onespiritpress@gmail.com

Table of Contents

To my three favorite people ~ Hana, Eli, and Colin~

" Have patience with everything unresolved in your heart and try to love the questions themselves, as if they were locked rooms, or books written in a very foreign language. Live the questions now."

Rainer Maria Rilke

"Never lose a holy curiosity." - Albert Einstein

Meet the Questions

Questions are the guts of life. I love them --especially the ones which make you think, which challenge and possibly generate a little disquiet. Perhaps in the uneasiness of questioning, a door cracks open and a fresh experience of the unimaginative wafts through. Questions are a road toward examination, the knowing of our self or another. They are a fundamental part of knowledge and wisdom. Perhaps not always appealing or reassuring, questions press upon us, and if we allow them, urge us to a deeper, more authentic place in ourselves.

Some of us shy away from questioning, beyond "what's for dinner?" and "did you walk the dog?" We fear the unknown, more arcane questions which conjure in our minds black holes we steer as far away from as possible. Asking questions reminds me I am committed to growing. I am changing. In that shift I can affect the world within --and sometimes--around me.

At times we can see more clearly through questioning. In other moments the questions continue to remain a mystery. Everyday prompts and insights, however, do avail themselves in the tiniest ways when we open ourselves to inquiry. Occurrences such as a dream, a chance meeting of someone who says the most appropriate thing, a new book offering a bit of wisdom, or a challenging life experience can unlock another opportunity. On these occasions, do we take time to wonder?

To question is 'to ask,' which, at its Old English origin, is 'to wish.' Ask is also synonymous with appeal and beseech. My favorite of these definitions (though they all hold a certain power) is 'to wish' because it begets the idea of something with yearning --perhaps even a hunger. When I perceive a question inside myself, I crave to know, to be in tune with the thought process that revolves around the unanswered. Like a mission I accept, the question becomes a new dynamic, ripe with potential access to the unknown and requiring earnest investigation.

Think about all the mechanical questions we respond to daily, such as, "What's your name and what do you do?" Consider the number of times you ask or are asked, "How are you?" While that question is loaded with buried treasure, most of us reply with a cursory, "Fine." We don't dig deep for HOW we truly are. Maybe we don't even know, simply because we don't attach enough importance to the interior questions of life, beginning with "Who am I?"; "Why am I?"; "Where do I fit?"

Confidence, like art, never comes from having all the answers; it comes from being open to all the questions. I appreciate artists, authors, explorers and philosophers who have posed questions that stretch the limits of my understanding. They have forged paths and pioneered in the struggle to be more within their human expression, by their questioning a different way. They have offered wisdom and beauty --often at a great cost-- in order to shine a light so I might risk a dream. Author Anais Nin claimed it required courage to live an expansive life. Sometimes an armor of that mettle is required to question ourselves in the midst of it, especially when there are times we feel as though we are barely hanging on.

As illustrated by many of these greats, life was often challenging and troubled in the pursuit of one's gift. Following Beethoven's premiere performance of his Ninth Symphony, he turned to his audience to see them applaud because he could no longer hear them. His genius required another element of invention: how to continue composing music without one's innate sense of hearing. Living in that quandary carried him a number of creative, albeit difficult, years and to our benefit, more of his lyrical expression. How then, as ordinary human beings, can we carry on when we find ourselves at an emotional or spiritual loss?

There is an art to asking questions and as in any creative presentation there are many versions. Free to move and change, be simple or complex, colorful, visceral, sometimes even silly, it is merely in the asking that questions form their magic. Similar to alchemy, we change the query to an active state, its life taking a shape we cannot always predict or expect.

Recently, Elizabeth, one of my elementary-aged grand-children sweetly asked me, "Don't you get sad living by yourself?" At that moment, emotion thumped a chord in my heart as I considered her thoughtful concern. Her act of wanting to know how I felt shifted me into an inner world in a way I couldn't have foreseen. Her innocent question reminded me that an essential part of asking a question is to do so from a place of respect.

Practicing this care through genshai --holding all others in their excellence and belittling no one including oneself-- is an important ingredient of the inquiry process. From there, inspiration leads into a progression that, for some of us, is almost second nature. I ask simply because I do not know --and I wish to know. Elizabeth's question became my own, ripe for honest conversation with a 9 year-old, as well as some serious, personal reflection.

Friends and family are familiar with my lines of questioning. I'm pretty certain I've seen an eye roll a time or two when I signal them with, "Okay, I have a question for you." Then again, I think they secretly like me to ask. I know they understand it's because I care. I value their thoughts.

Last summer, following a memorial service of a family friend, my adult children and I gathered with their spouses around a table with summer beverages and mightily open hearts. My question was, "What do you want people to remember about you?" Their sincere and thoughtful replies touched me very deeply: generosity in assisting others with less, being available and present to loved ones, deep commitment to one's spiritual path, helping youth believe in themselves through activity, motivation toward excellence and change were their responses. Perhaps the question offered moments to regard each other a little more, and interestingly enough, these traits and qualities were reflections of the gentle friend we'd lost. We had been witness to the remembrance of a life lived, and in consideration of his absence, we could mine the best of who we were in that moment.

Questions are mysterious pieces of the Self, constantly clarifying and building on our human nature. They are invaluable. Whatever your personal questions might be, ask them. Rouse them from their sleep as they move within your heart and mind. Take them into nature, work, adventure, silence and dreams. Let them bewilder, amuse and maybe even torment you. Journal them, sing and dance them. Wrestle with them. Consider them mentors and taskmasters.

Ask those questions of yourself and others. Grow with them like friends you cherish, letting them blossom slowly. Live the questions, in the light of day as well as during the darkest nights of the soul. Could it be in moments, weeks, years or even lifetimes, you might also live some of the answers?

"The world is but a school of inquiry."

Michel deMontaigne

"I don't know yet, but I'm working on it."

- Merrilee Parr

Who Am I?

Some time ago, I asked family and friends this question, as a survey: "Who are we in this complicated world?" The responses received were varied, from the esoteric to the technological. Philosopher, poet and Sufi mystic, Rumi, posed this question in the thirteenth century. His doctrines advocated tolerance, positive reasoning, goodness, charity and awareness through love. Rumi believed passionately in the use of music, poetry and dance as a path to the divine. His teachings represented a mystical journey of spiritual ascent. In one's personal walk of life, the seeker turned toward the truth and grew through love. At its highest, humanity was to serve without discrimination toward other beliefs, races, classes or nations. Am I --as part of humankind-- capable of such greatness, of such humility? Where and how do I begin?!

If I'm not a title, gender, ethnicity, familial tie or occupation, what am I? Where do I fit? What am I supposed to be doing? My curious nature delves into different possibilities of explanation, seeking answers to these questions. I search outside myself in people, places and things. I also look inside my heart and soul, paying attention to whichever insight makes itself clear. Intuition might guide me to turn at that traffic light, make that call, write that letter or respond to the offer made. What ensues from these ordinary experiences show me parts of myself. Pursuing the mainstream, alternative or combination thereof, I am incited by a force that drives me toward wanting to know. I find myself in relationships, jobs, lifestyles and interests that color the canvas of day-to-day. I endeavor to pay attention to the lessons illustrated in this painting (or not) depending on my state of awareness and willingness to find meaning in all of life.

Dreams challenge and excite me with their mixed up images and the curious. After the intensity of a nightmare, do I understand the panic of being pursued might actually be healing me? What do I need to wake up to? Confidence? Strength? Self-Reliance? Is the feeling of not being good enough, a burden I inherited from someone else and continue to place on myself? Has my mind summoned these inexplicable dream images in order to look more closely at something significant; something I don't recognize in my waking state? Fears that consume me with perceived failures and inadequacies actually may be the prompt to editing my personal story. "Dreams are illustrations…from the book your soul is writing about you," cites American playwright and 1983 Pulitzer Prize winner, Marsha Norman. Perhaps my nocturnal visions are yet another possibility for transformation, for pursuing individual and collective ambitions.

I assume nothing. I leap and trust the net will appear. I'm happy. I'm hopeless. There is incredible joy and good fortune. The dark nights of the soul are crushing and deep. I am shadow and light, all too human and all the while divine. I am no more or less than anyone else.

Is there an ascent to our living? How then do we carry on? How do we proceed toward truth? What is the truth anyway? Where do we find encouragement when catastrophic illness becomes a setback or divorce a constant battle of wills? Who decides loss or win? In a world fraught with destruction and impermanence, what do we really understand about our role in it all?

A wise, elderly friend's words reverberate in me: "What are your questions?" I continue to make a list. I gaze outward to consider myriad other perspectives, yet knowing it is my search alone to be no one but myself. As Oscar Wilde quipped, "...everyone else is already taken." I live all the moments, alone and with others whose stories are woven together with mine. I search, wonder and falter, but always keep asking. Isn't that all any of us can do?

"One must still have chaos in oneself to give birth to a dancing star."

- Friedrich Nietzsche

Pathfinder

Everything changes. What was once even partially secure will eventually no longer be: the good, the bad, the black, gray or white. All circumstances will change and change again. I've come to understand this dictum, overused and perhaps disbelieved by some, is an authentic truth. Sheryl Crow's words remind me: "Change will do you good."

How many of us want to buy that line? Which ones of us willingly trust-and-jump when life shifts and there is no choice but to change? Who among us will brave the doubt and uncertainty when the job doesn't support, the relationship fails, and terminal illness and death hasten us to the edge of our survival mode? Gilda Radner described this having to change as "delicious ambiguity" the not knowing, being in a place unaware of outcome --particularly one we desire.

I recently resigned a job as supervisory cook in a residential care home. After filling a file folder to an inch and a half thick of employment applications in a new city, I was called to Cherry Blossom, a cottage-like dwelling. I labored there for the better part of a year. My coworkers and 40+ senior residents were like a family all those months. I showed up early, chopped like a madwoman, provided nutrition where it had been lacking, offered attention in the spaces it was longed for.

The physical toll on my middle-aged (actually beyond) body became blatantly apparent when I hobbled instead of walking the evening hours following nine to ten hours of kitchen work. No amount of justifying I had work in a state where unemployment was high, fueled me to stay put and tough it out. I knew I had to forge another way. Being my own pathfinder into the future was imperative as I stepped out with ambiguity and question. How would I find my way? Would the bills get paid? Somehow the prospects didn't sound so delicious!

A close friend wrestled with similar choices about work she'd envisioned in a new, dynamic city which had lost its gleam and failed to provide adequately. Change was upon her as well, causing plenty of distress about what to do next. Which direction should she follow? "Leap and the net will appear" never sounded so poignant, as in this recent cross-road of now what?

In his book *Aspire*, Kevin Hall writes about our role as pathfinder, participating in the journey. French in origin, journee is defined as a day's travel. We humans (certainly this one), try to map out an entire life instead of the next few steps. We endeavor to control the visual of what we imagine we can or will create to sustain us. Choices and decisions become mind and gut wrenching. Waves of fear ripple through us as a mighty storm, and in our suffering to know 'what next?' we cease to trust our soul's map.

On which path do we honestly want to plant our feet? Is it one society, tradition or family has defined for us? Have we really taken the time to travel the unknown long enough to decipher what is genuine and necessary in our lives this moment? There comes a time when the choice is NO other choice but to step out.

Once I loved a man who told me he wasn't going to change; he liked the way he was. Changing seemed mainly my responsibility in the relationship. Amending who I was became the norm, for losing the connection to him would have been devastating to me. And for a time at the end, it was. I learned yet again that soul had invited me to grow and in doing so I had to wander a path that held uncertainties and supplementary pain. I was again called to the job of pathfinding, scouting and truly discovering what I was supposed to be doing at this point in my beyond-middle-aged life.

"Heaven embraces the horizon. No matter how jagged the profile, the sky faithfully conforms." Tao reminds us no matter what circumstances life may present we must bend and remain flexible to the circumstances. Knowing resistance was futile --and what we resist will persist-- I chose change. Eventually a satisfying job with ample hours, generous pay and less physical demand came my way. As far as I can tell, change *will* do you good!

"It is hearts breaking against the bodies of those we love."

- Terry Tempest Williams

Dispel the Pain

Pain is a four-letter word. Inflammatory, sometimes shocking and mood altering, it positions itself in our bones, our hearts, our thoughts and at times, our every movement. We become "overwhelmed by the sensation of vulnerability and fear" according to Mingyur Rinpoche. Our mistaken beliefs and skewed thinking take us on a roller coaster ride of the psyche. Climbing to dizzying heights of self-deprecation or narcissism (whichever fits the individual personality), and spiraling downward to perils of unflagging negative, nonproductive emotion, we stumble precariously through our lives. We struggle through loss of our true self, emotional flagellation or self righteousness in constant concert, as the pain increases and our need to control, desire to expand and subsequent perceived inadequacies rush us onward. We hurtle through space and time aching for relief. How do we assuage the agony in some small measure?

Once in a while, someone comes along to remind us we are not our pain. Perhaps a friend, a teacher, a child --even a stranger-- is the someone who shows up to reflect a determination to rise above, to literally see the light amidst the sting of suffering. A good friend of mine reminds me that, though the body may be ravaged by debilitating disease, the choice toward attitude of our experiences is always an option. She continually projects goodness, humor and interest toward others as her own body simultaneously continues to break down, nerve by nerve, immobilizing her action though never her spacious, bountiful heart.

Contrasting that expression of what I would call soul nature, another female in my world has made a choice toward blame, misery and a self-imposed prison. Through great tragedies that have befallen her, she has forged an armor and at times, a vitriol that seem only to have crushed her deeper into despair and longing. Unwilling, perhaps unable to move forward, she is trapped literally in an existence that is cloistered, angry and fearful. Is physical or emotional pain more profound, more damaging? Whose presence are we able to abide with and who needs our compassion more?

"Attitude is a little thing that makes a big difference," offered Winston Churchill. A levelheaded elder friend of mine with a sense of humor used to tell me, "have a pity party and get over it; life's short." Some spiritual teachings advocate compassion and loving-kindness, based on the understanding all of us want to be happy and free of suffering. While the idea of getting over something as great as multiple sclerosis or tragic sudden death are nearly unthinkable, are we able to at least face the idea a tiny step toward it is possible? Can we illuminate the positive in some minute way?

Carl Jung believed "the sole purpose of human existence is to kindle a light in the darkness of mere being." Is that light --the soul-- enough to remind us we are more than these bodies and minds? With these faculties, do we have the capacity to bring compassion to ourselves and others? My dear sister-friend, Melissa, continues to spread her wealth of brightness and humility, inspiring my deep admiration of her life's example. She fuels my purpose toward an optimistic outlook of loving-kindness, empathy and true spirit --and in those moments, freedom from suffering and pain.

My Questions

"Great perils have this beauty that they bring to light the fraternity of strangers."

- Victor Hugo

In the Middle

Early Sunday morning, a bomb hit the building next door. Of course, it wasn't a real explosion, but the intense sound jolted me from my place at the computer. Decked in floral pajamas and green polka dotted fleece robe, I dashed to the front window. Like Gladys the Nosey Neighbor, I peered out to see if my curbside car had been hit by some inattentive driver. Just last week, I'd discovered the first of several side-swipe marks on the bumper of my penny-colored vehicle. "Don't sweat the small things," popped into my head about the time my eyes caught sight of one car in the yard and another, with a turned-up lip of a hood, idled in the intersection.

Pema Chodron believes we should "experience our lives this moment." At 8:30 a.m., when that reverberation inundated my senses, adrenalin coursed through me. Something unusual had occurred and not what most of us hoping for an easy-like-Sunday-morning would fancy. While my square road master sat precisely as I had left it, the junction of the two streets was filled with a crumpled front-end car and a pink-shirted, cell phone talking man pacing the blacktop. Just a few feet away stood an apparent mother with her young offspring wrapped tightly in her embrace. She appeared to be surveying her own car that had levitated off the street and into the flower bed. Without considering my crazy morning garb, I grabbed my cell phone, threw open the door and ran down the stairs toward the scene of chaos.

The females, indeed mother and daughter, had emerged shaken from their car tangled with the front porch of the apartment building next to mine. Up the curb, across the sidewalk, through the brief plot of grass, their car had cruised, its final resting place atop spring daffodils and ja-ponica. The midsize sedan look as devastated and rumpled --air bags deployed, interior possessions tossed about-- as the mother with her panic stricken child by her side. The driver, no doubt husband and father, showed his fear with an air of agitation and embarrassment. His concern over getting to their destination seemed to take precedence over his pos-sible mistake at the wheel and his shaken family.

Having recently taken a CPR class I quickly assessed the situation for safety, and then walked to the older female who now sat with the girl on the curb. The youngster held the side of her face in her hand. Touching the woman gently on her shoulder, I asked, "Are you okay?" A nervous smile crossed her face and a quiet, verbal assurance to the affirmative told me they were certainly better off than their vehicle.

During the moments that followed as the family waited for emergency service assistance, I reemerged from my apartment with a bag of frozen berries for the young girl's face, a Bach Flower remedy for trauma, and a plush blanket grabbed from a chair in the living room. I draped the cover over their huddled together shoulders, and like Siamese twins, their outside hands wrapped around one another, grasping the mantle of warmth. Offering drops of flower essence, they accepted its anointment on their wrists without hesitation. A whispered "thank you" was barely audible --a sigh of relief and comfort more noticeable. Chilled, shaking, and obviously in shock, mother and daughter sat silently.

While matters of immobile autos, friends to pick up the now-stranded, and the burden of responsibility between the male drivers all took place, we three female strangers garnered a moment of quiet conversation. It included the everyday, soccer, school and friends while deflecting the obvious and illuminating providence. Time stood still. Was this quiet grace among strangers?

Ralph Waldo Emerson said "place yourself in the middle… without effort…" Could this be how we honor life around us? As the mother remained calm in attending her daughter, EMTs discerned need, and my nosey, neighbor self held council with strangers, synchronicity wedged a path in the center. Perhaps a bit of the miraculous occurred that Sunday morning when car met concrete, and humans converged in an unplanned assembly of fate which could have turned tragic. I don't believe this was small stuff either, but it never is when we reside at the heart of each moment, giving to others and thereby ourselves, in the miraculous coincidences of life.

"In the works of man as in those of nature, it is the intention which is chiefly worth studying."

Johann Wolfgang von Goethe

Survivor --
The Real Stories

The doctor's three-month death sentence provoked her. She admitted frankly, it pissed her off. Who was this man telling her to get her affairs in order like the business of living is any small matter? Her life was capacious and expressed itself constantly through her family, friends, and art. A feistier, more engaging and present human being you weren't likely to meet. Randa was the epitome of living a colorful life. She planted varied shades of pink and iridescent blue bowling balls along with tomatoes and cosmos in her garden. Friends and family had the good fortune to be recipients of her exquisitely painted landscapes, and her artistic whimsy was further shared with children when she volunteered at our kids' elementary school.

Randa entered a room with confidence and command. She was witty, interested, direct and unfiltered. One evening while delightfully immersed in wine, conversation and women friends, she bluntly told a peer at the table her current love interest was a crazy mistake! She could've been asking to pass the salt.

At home with four children to mother, there was no time for dying. This verdict of the end was a challenge and one she would rise to with the power and creativity that was intrinsic in her. Statistics like promises are quite often broken, and shatter those numbers she did for eight more spirited years --not without trials, pain, and moments of profound sadness. Could I have mustered the courage I witnessed so valiantly in her?

Unlike family or friends who ultimately leave, there are the ones who persist and convey a different stamina. Fortitude through daily anguish, caring for their beloved --their husbands-- depicted the stoicism of two such women who chose a difficult path, with a similar conclusion. At home, able bodied and dedicated to their spouses, they administered both medication and love with diligence and a perseverance that exemplified the affection in their hearts. Devastated, exhausted and knowing death would explicably dash their world, tears were shed in solo performance. Hope was eked out. It was lost.

When the final days arrived and their life-partners were gone, their mourning already in progress, took on the valor of moving ahead. Alone, raising children as well as self, and without drowning in despair, these women became more. One furthered her education to support singularly her four offspring. She lived into old age; gritty, outspoken, and with genuine loyalty toward those she trusted most. In her later years she grew heirloom tomatoes and tiny French green beans in her garden. Tareytons were her cigarette of choice and the pot of coffee was always on. Margaret loved a good story and her own were filled with the fascinating events of an 85-year life well lived.

The other was a master demonstration of kindness constantly in service, composed at her near-retirement age. Traveling from the Philippines many years before as a young bride-to-be, Arsenia had exchanged long letters and fallen in love with the man who became her husband. His illness fell upon them swiftly, but her care and devotion were solid throughout the final months of his life. When I met her later as an employee in an elder care residence, her hard work and integrity continued to define her selfless character and strength of will. She looked forward to returning to her homeland where she would live out her single life close to family and longtime friends.

These courageous women have been guides to me, unwavering and extraordinary. They have embodied the tenacity and will to rise above, to divine their deepest selves in a time that was their nadir. How could they possibly accomplish what they did while traversing the valleys of deep sorrow and hopelessness? Tao te Ching tells us "Stand at the precipice of that existential darkness and call into the void: it will surely answer." Who answers? Who directs? Why me? Why not? Promises of hope are gifts that exist in a surreal world of their own, and so often reclaimed as prerequisite for learning. Can we live as if everything is a miracle? Can we anticipate it is worth the effort? Is there any other choice?

"…a mother's love endures through all."

- Washington Irvington

Alive With Light

Who among us are mothers? The very fabric, cellular and core level of a mother can be likened to nothing else. Does anything run as deeply caring, so teeming with love as the passion a mother has for her children? The bond many of us as mothers have to our sons and daughters begins, certainly as they incubate within our bodies. Our connection may have no beginning or end, but simply be a shared strand of some mystery only understood in quiet moments.

For the better part of one year women bear the significance of a growing life --physically, emotionally, and spiritually. While swollen ankles and roiling stomachs may wreak havoc, this child is a blessing at the least; a miracle at most. We feel them move, sense their development, anticipate their impending emergence. As our body changes to accommodate them, we begin to understand, on a deeper level, only a few of the countless ways we will support them through our lives together. Beginning with them taking what they need from our bodies to yielding to their exodus into the world, we endure the combined pain. As the miraculous occurs and our child lies vulnerable in our protective arms, the journey of lifelong love continues in earnest.

Throughout the years of nurturing these loves and challenges of our life, we remain attached to them with devotion as well as occasional trepidation. We stand in awe and wonder at the potential of their existence. Equally, we comprehend the pain in the world that will not elude them. At the center of our human mothering, we know it is not, cannot, be our responsibility to keep it from them. The greater unknown in becoming who they are is out of sight of our mind's eye. Often we cannot direct their well being anymore than we can change the earth's spinning on its axis. As mothers, perhaps we are merely stewards to their story, their destiny --certainly their place in our heart.

When fate interrupts the sacredness of the mother-child bond, devastation occurs. Like rock striking glass, fragmentation unparalleled shatters our core. We are brought to our knees by the irreverent, the seizing of that which is closest to our soul. No greater sorrow can befall us as mothers than losing the flesh of our flesh, heart of our heart --a son or daughter.

We mourn with a friend whose loss is shocking and visceral. Our own hearts are broken open by this grief so immense one surely cannot contain it all. We understand the tears, the disbelief, and impossible hope that it all be a passing nightmare. We give silent thanks for the momentary wellbeing of our own offspring. Is there any salve to soothe a broken spirit when the unimaginable --death-- happens? Will the sheer emptiness and shock wave rippling through our core diminish enough that we might draw breath again? Can a loss so immense be understood at a human level?

Our soul, the eternal part of who we are, calls upon us to unequivocally surrender to the mysterious. We are asked from that mystery to hold a space for the tragedies of physical life that makes no sense. To do so, we must call upon grace to endure our anguish. Perhaps in those moments when we are able, we are "alive with light" as Jeffrey Douglass writes in *Living From Your Soul*. As we access an instant of openness to the divine, we may also perceive a union with the one we have lost. The cord, which began as an umbilical, has transformed into the unseen, no longer earthly. Yet, it is genuine, powerful, not easily severed --a gift from one soul to another.

"When I die, I shall soar with angels, and when I die to the angels, what I shall become you cannot imagine." Rumi tells us the soul is our spring of harmony and all possibility. The world of spirit is "real, undivided, dynamic, creative and free of limitation," writes Depak Chopra. The ingredients for living and dying are many, and must surely be determined singularly from our universal selves --all too human and simultaneously born of light.

"I am a piece of the puzzle, discovering where I best fit."

- Cheri Calvert

Bearer of Love

A brief stopover in small town USA revived her broken heart and prepared a toehold for the next leg of the journey. Big city. Bigger dreams. Daring enough to just go! Like uneven pieces to a jigsaw puzzle, we turned and re-turned that heavy, propane grill every which way to fit it in the U-Haul. You wouldn't have thought that extra foot of height in the metal box --only costing double the price-- would've made that much difference. Next time less coffee and more math consideration!

The monster barbeque grill would remain behind in the nearly empty garage keeping counsel with the new renter's trundle. The haul-it-yourself wagon was loaded to the gills now with bequeaths of collected treasures meant for family members several hundred miles east, a pit stop on the road to new life. Riches only its owner and new recipients could value included a cache of love tied in tiny ribbons and new-born sizes. Was she running away again? Would the deep grief carved in her heart ever scar over and heal?

The more important, live cargo -- also on the way to new environs-- was furry, mightily odorous and adored beyond measure. Nearly four hundred pounds of canine were stowed in the black and mucky Suburban, its cavern open and accessible to one-sided conversation and love vibrations. One of the furred passengers was female, a redhead always in the navigator's seat riding tall in a protective, shot-gun position. This load of wealth, better known as Thor, Wilma Jean, and Travis, was the saving grace and driving force --though not behind the wheel-- fortifying the human traveler to persist. Proceeding with another dose of letting go, she laid to rest a ration of emotion and fractured dreams like a dog's chew bones and favored toys in the soft, autumn earth. How many of us have shed a tear or two alongside a dream not destined to be?

Leaving town after a short stint in the northwest, her moniker would be remembered in every way upbeat, go-to-it and genuine. Her spirit was as beautiful and innocent as youth, her mind sharp like Wisconsin cheddar. The food description was an appropriate one, since she lived on cheese and what it covered --mainly pizza. Though cooking was not her forte, authenticity, curiosity for life, and wonder at all that was good were just a few of her precious assets. She hugged as a longtime friend, spread humor and care with abandon, and never assumed the worst before the best. Tami was a bearer of love, a soul whose grace and dignity still outshines most.

Who could've imagined our paths would cross? Why? Her friendship was a surprise, but soul shows great deference to heart connections, sisterhood and to the everyday miracle of chance. Appreciation of a friend recognized in a random moment is a sacred experience akin to a beautiful mosaic. Its parts are intricate, vibrant and full of potential. Now thousands of miles away, her heart resides, piecing together a new career, home and expression. Her spirit, however, remains woven with mine, its elements able to withstand change, individuality and separation, knowing someday the story will continue.

Not only are longtime friendships accomplished through chance meetings, but the momentary, even vicariously realized love-bearers come along in the most extraordinary ways. "She stuck her hand right in the wound. She saved my life!" These words were passing conversation heard by my three grandchildren and me as we rode on the streetcar last summer. Having recently left Powell's Bookstore with their newly purchased storytelling works, the G-kids were now riveted to this elderly man's hair raising tale. His narrative went on to depict a horrible fall he had taken, incurring a deep gash on his forehead. Blood poured from his face and the woman, whom he described as an angel, came instantly to his rescue, curbing the flow with her hand positioned literally inside the cut. A life was saved by the openness of a complete stranger. As fate would have it that sunny day the stranger was a not only an angel, but a nurse.

Portland has a significant population of homeless within its city limits. Many of these men and women struggle to find food, shelter and sanity intact on any given day. I had the opportunity to occasionally visit with one of them when I undertook some landscaping duties for the landlord of the apartment I rented. Linden's route for collecting recyclables included the courtyard where I labored mowing, weeding and watering. On our first meeting, he smiled as he removed his hat and politely asked, "Ma'am, would you mind if I took the glass from the bins?" So taken by his gentle courtesy, I beamed my own response, "You go right ahead." After he found what he was looking for, we chatted amiably for several minutes before he wished me a good day and walked away. I saw Linden several times during my landscaping stint. Once, he offered to help me move a large bag of compost. He always graciously asked before searching the bins for glass. His kindness was palpable.

Most of us bear love. Don't we all bear pain as well? It's part of our human condition, a duality of life in the physical realm. Can we see in this collective puzzle we all play a part; we are all the same? No matter what circumstances life has dealt us, each has dreams. For many those dreams are often dashed by misfortune and loss. However, on any given day, a dog-loving-Blondie, an angel, a gentle man --fellow humans-- appear out of nowhere and we are changed by their magnificent presence. Isn't it moments like these, all the pieces seem to fit together so easily?

Love Notes to Self

"Let us turn life into an adventure of absorbing interest."

- Edward Bach

Possessed

Socrates considered it a gift, an inner voice he adhered to without question in all matters. It warned of unforeseen danger or poor judgment. Plato understood there existed a spirit separate from man, yet assigned to him throughout his lifetime, rather like a guardian angel. Some psychology purports that in our individuation --development toward wholeness-- this power assists us in overcoming obstacles. Ironically, this inexplicable force may also summon the stumbling blocks of defeat, death, or illness which rouse us to the edge of our habitual routines and accepted convictions.

As we evolve throughout our lives, we witness a truer identity of personal strength, passion and vision for life's purpose which can often involve risk and the less traveled path. Who or what is this invisible power, claimed to drive us forward? Could it be what the ancients described as our daimon, a numinous presence, divine urge, deep intuition?

I recently encountered Christopher in a small social group at a local eatery. His quiet natured belied his intrepid story of leaving behind work as a successful, east coast, attorney for an emotionally richer experience in the northwest. Not only did he brave a significant life change and initiate a brand new career working in the field of autism, he took more time for regular travel and exploration. With thoughtful forewarning to his employer, he readies for a randomly selected destination every two years. I imagine this is how he soothes his soul, governs his artistic expression and allows universal intelligence to play itself through him.

Remarkably, I was in touch that night with three others who were living their dreams as an acupuncturist, private school educator and small business owner. These individuals were pursuing what moved them with less heed toward making big dollars. Is this a transformation of the American dream, a pursuit of passion? Could it be an inner calling we are destined to discover if we open ourselves to all the possibilities?

My youngest son personifies the phrase 'living out loud.' His personal strength is robust, his zeal luminous. Recently boarding a helicopter with several other thrill seekers, he landed (more than once) atop a peak in the Purcell Mountain range of British Columbia, with a plan to ride the summit. Imagine "Lucy in the Sky with Diamonds" invoking a scene of sparkling "blower" snow, azure horizons, scalloped downhill tracks, speed and exhilaration. I didn't need to board that chopper --nor would I ever have the nerve-- to feel stirred by the magic of those moments. Watching his snowboarding video-journal generated tears of amazement and the con-

stant verbalization, "Oh my God!" Colin's divine urge to really be in this world through epic adventure incites my spirit.
He models a life led by daimon, one rich with potential and
wonder.

  Thomas Moore describes the daimon as a primal, creative
desire, perhaps directing our character, style and destiny. Living with this principle often requires whimsy, audacity, and
spontaneity. Do some of us call it crazy sometimes?! English
novelist, Margaret Drabble, declares "when nothing is sure,
everything is possible." Stepping outside the box isn't easy
for many people. Others consider this their norm. When
the daimon pounces on the psyche and opens a gateway to
the soul rousing and cajoling "something incredible is wait-
ing to be known." Carl Sagan lived this creed, and was perhaps spurred on to brilliant, scientific eminence by his own
daimon. In our more modest and less systematic lives, can
we simply remain alert to signs and intuitions until we are incited by our personal spirit guide? After all, possession could
well be nine tenths of the law --of a human BE-ing, that is.

"He who is devoid of the power to forgive is devoid of the power to love."

- Martin Luther King, Jr.

Another Cheek

Forgiveness. How do we wrap our minds around a concept such as this one when the depravity of a mentally unbalanced human infects the innocence of a child? How can we control our outrage after the tears have wrested every ounce of energy we possess?

A recent news article reported the arrest of an east coast pediatrician who had over 400 cases of child abuse charges brought against him. In our midst: predator, monster, sociopath, all titles bestowed on a human capable of such horrific and loathsome behavior. Unfortunately in our society today, this conduct has been publicized the world over in walks of life from the ordinary to the religious --parents to priests. When we aim at living a purposeful life and hit a stone wall of violence, how do we proceed?! Surely there is no capacity to anoint human brutality against a child with a gift as sacred as forgiveness.

Andrea began with a grandmother who adored and sheltered her, offering nurture in all the ways newborns deserve --for half a year. Just six months was the amount of time she would have in childhood to feel loved, safe and understood. What followed, at the hands of others in the next many years, were patterns of cruelty so immense we could only imagine them because they were broadcast on national news.

While many cannot fathom these unspeakable crimes against children, others have experienced them firsthand. We have lived through inexorable fear and anxiety of the door opening at night, someone stealing into our space and ultimately into our personal being. Our only protection was a shift of consciousness, a removal from the part of us being overpowered by another human being. As time elapsed in that hell, we learned to forget, to block the memory of experience. We helplessly witnessed in ourselves multiple personalities, attitudes of rebellion, anxiety and deep depression --anything that might quell our understanding we were prisoners being held with no foreseeable release.

As we grew into adulthood, each of us battled with mental and emotional demons. Nightmares, unexplained anger and emotional lethargy prompted ideas of self destruction. We labored more years at further cost to heal ourselves privately in order to maintain normalcy in relationship, family and the everyday. Taking two steps ahead, we also took as many back, failing again and again, losing ground in the memory of a wound so profound. Though our human spirit is said to be strong, is it not our soul that urges us back? We pick up the pieces deliberately, worn out yet determined to restore life. What keeps us from resentment and bitterness? How do we honor our spirit of resilience and calibrate this darkness to some measure of light?

I recall a shy, soft-spoken, girl from my days as a classroom, volunteering mother. Now a young adult, Brandy exhibited an unbeknownst heroism when she and her boyfriend noticed through an uncovered window two small children trapped in a filthy room. They had no clothes or blankets and their tiny bodies were covered with excrement, bruises, and infected wounds. I believe when she and Anthony decided to report this appalling condition to the police, some of Brandy's personal darkness was spun into light.

Her own childhood and home circumstances had been questionable, illicit, and filthy. At the time, I reported her situation to the school counselor and classroom teacher. Our family invited her into our home and lives on many occasions. Perhaps those small measures --meals, play time, walks on our property-- offered some ballast to the system's and parental inadequacies. Her subsequent survival and concern years later became a turning point in the lives of those two preschool-aged girls. Did she also glimpse her own ill-fated childhood in the shared rescues of those little ones?

Psychology 101 states that the majority of people will not respond to a threatening situation they witness. They either do not want to get involved or believe the burden of responsibility is someone else's. It is a side of human behavior, especially in groups, where the vulnerable remain unprotected. When we ignore the defenseless, how do we forgive ourselves later on? Forgiving the wrong-doer is no less an undertaking. I have questioned my own capacity to pardon, again and again.

Author and theologian, Lewis Smedes believed "to forgive is to set a prisoner free and discover that the prisoner was you." As we start to see the light of freedom, we gradually file away the numerous titles we've self-proclaimed: unworthy, hopeless, bad. Over the years of struggling to heal from such odious treatment, we turn off this internal dialogue of further denigration. We cease salting the wounds with the persistent belief that these hurts are who we are. We take up our own cause, a necessary one because the repetitive chatter in our brains has been on the repeat mode a long time.

Being present to others who suffer, to intend that our life's trajectory blesses, and open our hearts are just a few ways we find cure. Not without doing our own work, not without setting boundaries when necessary, and not without a bucket load of inner soul searching and forgiving ourselves. Could it be, the moment we acknowledge we are both the forgiver and the forgiven, that true healing occurs? Our greatest work could well be our darkest, and the illumination realized might be our soul holding the torch.

More Questions

"The noble soul has reverence for itself."

- Friedrich Nietzsche

Look and Lift

Guatemala, plus five brothers, no showers, non-existent technology, and a huge measure of compassion recently engendered change through altruism. Family of man, literally, embarked on a journey to beautiful, if not harsh, mountain villages in Central America. Over 60% of the population lives in poverty. Only a small portion of their land is arable and malnutrition is prevalent. The mission was to assist, build, and thereby improve the lives of the residents living in this bleak setting of lack and need. The project, intended by a small church in northern Idaho, fell on the heels of the country's common, natural disasters --a tropical storm and volcanic eruption. Two of those five brothers traveling to make a difference were immediately close to my heart, and when they set out, my juxtaposed feelings of apprehension and pride were immense.

In *Ordinary Grace* Kathleen Brehony illustrates numerous displays of good-deed-doing by everyday people, from the humblest to the more privileged strata of humanity. Her research as a clinical psychologist has led her toward acknowledging the principle that goodness clearly outweighs evil in our basic human nature. She cites that for "every instance of violence or greed there are thousands of acts of benevolence and tolerance." We all know the negative ones, for our media bombards us with these incidents of aggression on a daily basis. Where are the tales of everyday compassion that exist in our world? From what part of us, as mere mortals, do these acts of goodwill originate, and why? Is there a greater human or spiritual context from which these noble actions are often quietly performed?

The long held belief by some religious followers that human beings are born with original sin seems puritanical and limited. Some studies of human development, on the other hand, tout the power of nature and nurture as a determinant of one's virtuous behaviors. That possibility has been further supported by highly esteemed philosophers and theologians who assert humans are born neither good nor bad, but have the innate capacity for both. Perhaps more profoundly, developmental psychology is affirming through research that a predisposition toward positive behavior is present in humans. Neurological research has opened similar doors into a biology of empathy that is regulated by the amygdala, memory and emotion processor of the brain.

In the documentary *Oh My God*, a young boy smiles timidly from his hospital bed in an oncology unit. His face is serene, his head shiny and devoid of hair. Chemotherapy has been his routine. He responds without hesitation when asked if he had one wish, what it would be. The reply: "I wish all the wars and fighting in the world would stop." This demonstration of what we call altruism --unselfish concern for others-- is what sociologists are concluding is a measure of our basic human nature, one which begins at a very young age.

These Guatemala-bound men, some with families, others younger just beginning their adult lives, traveled thousands of miles to a country having recently experienced not only a volcanic eruption, but a tropical storm and a massive sinkhole that gulped down a factory. Was this a foolish mission? Having made their plans in advance to give whatever aid they could to two small villages outside Guatemala City, these five brothers had been on hold to see if the airport would re-open post disasters, allowing them the opportunity to undertake their intentions. In short order, destiny sent them on their way!

Mixing sand, concrete, and precious water, they formed their own blocks, erecting simple stoves to be used by families for the meal preparation of their meager stores. Wide-eyed, bedraggled children, grateful mothers, and austere living conditions with fields of struggling vegetation enveloped this lot of noble souls. Positive regard, camaraderie and connection to Spirit were equally present. Setting aside personal lives they labored for a week, keeping their eyes on the goal and their hearts in the toil of making the villagers' lives incrementally better.

Perhaps part of reaching out to others, whether next door or in the next country, is a matter of simply paying attention to the intrinsic kindness inside us. In so doing, can we connect at a level of human reality, a significant place of association and understanding? Rebecca West believes "life ought to be a struggle of desire toward adventures whose nobility will fertilize the soul." Can we find our own souls perched at the edge of a divinity that fills us, and if we allow it, let it guide our actions toward a reverence for all life?

Two of those young men, five brothers from different parents, returned worn, beard-clad and deeply moved by their experience in Central America. My initial feeling of apprehension was relieved when I knew the young men were deplaning on familiar ground. Pride stepped aside for the incredible respect I felt about their journey of aid. Side by side with others in an extraordinary grace, lives were altered: the villagers of San Antonio, Liquidambar, and two of those particular sons originating from my own family of man.

Notes

"Each of us is a creatively different and complete icon of the cosmos."

- Mary Ellen Rodda

Impact Expansion

Spreading arms open wide, she belts out the latest, self written words of little girl wisdom. Soft curls bounce and deep brown eyes glisten as she sings for all she's worth. Laura knew at an early age she had something inside her, calling to make its way out into the world. Despite her sister's teasing and sisterly pronouncement she couldn't sing at all, she indeed found her way into the realm of musical performance. While in secondary school auditioning for Voices of Harmony, Laura was the only freshman selected to perform with the group. Many years later, with her own inimitable expression of song, she uplifts, inspires, and literally brings the individual to the magic of music with her soulful sounds.

As an activity director in a small, residential home, Laura's guitar work and sweet voice are a source of pure pleasure to the seniors living there. One or two of the gentlemen may well harbor a crush on her. When she gets her groove on at a local club, her bluesy tone and newfound lyricist talent rock the house. Do we pay attention to the call of our soul inviting us to tap our creative intellect and long held dreams? Or do we follow the conventional path because it is more practical, dutiful, or secure?

Miriam, another brilliant musician, could have heeded her father's well intended advice to pursue education with the objective of a well-paying, more mainstream occupation. Initially she did adhere to that counsel, respecting and loving the insight of her parent. As time went on and her academic endeavors led to receiving double collegiate awards for writing, Miriam gave herself permission to finally believe in her song writing ability. The universe opened doors for her, one after another, and she walked through them producing music shaped from a enthusiasm long felt. For now, her day job as a massage therapist is my good fortune. Tomorrow, I picture Miriam touring with her band and spreading harmony like honey; baby steps on a multi-layered journey.

Harmony expresses itself in other, less noticeable melodies as well. Within these city limits, many streets are traversed by those who have nowhere to call home. What they own is carried on their back or pushed in a shopping cart ahead of them. Piled, stored, stacked and well covered --some with bells and whistles, others minimally adorned-- transitory lives are self contained. They are different; they are the same: human.

At a local laundromat, many of these men and women gather to wash their few items of clothing. Alongside them, I've witnessed them sorting their whites meticulously, folding dried shirts gently, and speaking kindly when addressed by myself or another. The owner of this bustling business calls them his friends. One day, I heard the hearty laughter of the owner as he offered one of the men a soda. The street man was attempting to vend a half bottle of laundry soap for a couple of dollars. The business owner, knowing the money would most likely go toward the purchase of alcohol, withheld judgment as he offered the canned soda as a thirst quenching beverage instead. This generous-hearted citizen exchanges conversation, humor, and some of his daily profits to assist in keeping his fellow human beings in fresh clothing; what he considers a basic need. Is this unique soul's creative expression of giving exerting a positive influence in the world?

Our gifts, passions, and values are diverse. Yet, in the mix of those talents and kind hearts, we often discover a story of who we are at our finest. Oregon's Willamette University asserts in their school's motto: "Not unto ourselves alone are we born." Shall we take responsibility for our destiny by committing ourselves to small acts of positive effect using our abilities, benevolence, risk, and generosity? In opening doors for our fellow man or woman, we radiate an energetic signal that has great potential. Whether we follow our instincts and thoughtfully share an innate talent which uplifts, or bolster another's life by offering a basic need, we acknowledge a kindred spirit in the circle of humanity. What often originates from a higher place in one person culminates as a blessing for someone else. The various tunes of our individual I AM expression call us. Can we hear? Do we acknowledge? And for all the Laura's and Miriam's of life, "let's give it up" (round of applause, please) for the power of passion shared!

"The purpose of life is a life of purpose."

- Robert Byrne

Your Mission,
Should You Choose

Film has always been a favorite pastime, its big screen effect pulling me into the characters' experiences and emotions. Recently, *Conviction* captured my attention with its true tale element. The main actors portrayed siblings, having formed a close bond through the trials of an alcoholic, abusive and absent-parent childhood. When the brother of the pair is prosecuted for murder and sentenced to life in prison, his sister literally makes it her life's mission to free him. She does this at an extreme cost to her marriage and family. Perhaps though, not to herself as she upgrades her high school drop-out status to that of an attorney at law. For eighteen long years she endures obstacles and heartache to liberate her brother from a brutal crime verdict she is convinced he is innocent of committing.

What in us drives us toward this kind of sacrifice? Is it merely the love we feel for another human being? Is it our sense of justice and doing the right thing? Does purpose play a role in the choices we make toward living our lives with integrity? Why is this present in some and lacking in others?

One of my son's friends recently returned from several months in Ghana. She worked in a refugee camp, assisting mothers and young children in simple yet profound ways. I imagine her appearance as a tall, light-haired, blue eyed woman being the equivalent to an angelic presence amidst the individuals and families. Grace flowed through her as she interacted with children, aware of their needs and immersing herself in their austere lives. She worked side-by-side with mothers cooking meals from foods shipped to them from aid programs. She explored language with them. Hannah had been moved to study African culture with the intention of giving herself to something greater, the need of another. Perhaps she developed a propensity toward an open-handed life by the model of her parents, who worked with the Peace Corps. Her own inherent compassion and curiosity urges her forward. Many lives, including her own, have been shaped by this abundance of good which she expresses through serving.

How to live is different to each of us. As truth can be explored in a multi-facet of ways, so can living a conscious life. "Providing assistance is an act of spiritual alchemy in which you transfer energy or grace to someone else." Carolyn Myss' words echo a truth in the milieu of our human condition. In attending to the needs of others, can we find reason, purpose for our existence? In Viktor Frankl's *Man's Search for Meaning* where life in concentration camps consisted of horror and death, there still existed kindness and selflessness. A few

54

of the prisoners gave up their paltry scraps of bread to those who suffered more and this sacrifice, Frankl believed, was an expression of man's choice of action. Is this part of the 'spiritual freedom' he spoke of that sustained prisoners through daily agonies?

Do we understand our deeds are the fabric of our existence, something that makes life meaningful and purposeful? When we pay attention, we may find our conviction of purpose expressing itself in smaller ways --holding a door, encouraging words, advocating for someone, levity with a stranger, a thank you. No matter the example, conviction's potency can alter the course of reality. In the movie *Conviction*, as well as in real life, dignity of action can set us all free.

"All you need is love."

- Paul McCartney/John Lennon

Learn How to Be You

The Beatles, great icons of our musical history sing us a lullaby. Their words circulate inside us with the single most valuable resource granted us. Love. The refrain, "all you need is love," has been a mantra to many of us over the years. When we felt at our lowest or highest in emotion or event, we harkened back to that love. Perhaps we reveled in it, as well as called upon it to save us from emotional drowning. At other times we may have cursed it, given up ever finding it. We possessed it and we lost it --or so we thought.

Does love truly go missing? Becoming an active --if not inadvertent-- participant, recently in someone else's private world made me wonder. While walking home in Northwest Portland, I caught sight and sound of a young couple in a highly animated argument. In a matter of seconds, the scene unfolded before my eyes and ears as I continued my fast-paced trek homeward. A young female was highly incensed by something, and no sooner had she uttered words, her male partner was on the ground.

Dread instantly filled me as I continued to gain in proximity to their volatile space. Why hadn't I taken a different route? What also engulfed me immediately after the gripping alarm, were the words: "all you need is love." I even began to quietly sing those words until I was upon the two rabble-rousers and within view of another woman, just steps away. As I greeted her, she exclaimed, "Kids!" Then almost pleading, she asked, "Ma'am, if he hits her will you call the police?" Without missing a beat --still feeling that all we need is love-- I turned my head toward the youthful two, catching them in an instantaneous and hearty embrace. Relieved by the sudden turn of emotional behavior, I replied to the nervous mother figure, "They're ok; they've got love."

The beauty of irritation turning to affection (if only in that moment) was a pretty picture --a gift to observe. Do you believe in coincidence or the universe's power to change in a moment? Eden Ahbez asserts "the greatest thing you'll ever learn is just to love and be loved in return." We humans can often be pretty dense when it comes to heeding that message. For some, the act of loving without constraints is the challenge; for others, it is in the act of receiving without similarly wanting to control the situation.

Several months into their connection, Susan's usually thoughtful gentleman appeared in a state of chaos at a mutual friend's home for dinner. Having had a "few beers with friends" beforehand, he had difficulty carrying on a coherent conversation and his attempts to balance his dinnerware were muddled. My friend was taken aback. This blatant lack of sound judgment toward personal conduct was upsetting to say the least. Perhaps it wasn't the first time, as she mindfully thought back to other incidents in their togetherness. Excesses had come and gone; she'd explained them away as high energy. He ran a very successful business, after all. He was a passionate person, giving 110% to whatever struck his curiosity.

How do we decipher the difference between real love and neediness? How do we fill the hole in our wounded hearts when we've suffered aloneness and disregard? Love isn't always rose-colored. It takes effort and a diligence for it to thrive. We give. We take. Do we also learn from our history? This doesn't mean we wallow in its hurt, cling to its pain, or obsessively be critic to what went awry. Though, I've done all these! Self reflection, however, is generally a wise choice. What attracts us to certain personalities, events and places? Just what is our soul trying to highlight in the midst of our life experiences?

My friend engages in an internal debate between the belief she judges her companion and honoring her own sense of moral standard. She struggles with not wanting to be alone --her friend's presence warmly filling much of her life-- and listening intently to her inner voice. In loving another sometimes we place ourselves in the back seat, disregarding our deeper understanding. If we are to live honorably with others, wouldn't it be prudent to start with ourselves? Love is what we need, but not at the cost of falling asleep to "you can learn how to be you in time." Love begins inside each one of us and spirals into a collective. How do we linger long enough at that sacred source of our own being, honoring the whispers of truth, and stay vigilant to becoming an equal part of that thing called Love?

Self Observation

When you're finished changing, you're finished."

- Benjamin Franklin

The Space
You Occupy

Five people in my immediate world have died in the last two months. They all slipped away during the night; they had already departed when 911 was called and responded minutes later. Bodies no longer wondrous with life, let go of earthly hold. Souls tireless and bright uttered their final messages --silent words of release and love. Somewhere in the years they exacted from life, this quintet of elders (one at the seasoned age of 101) lived. Through struggle, focus, and often sheer will, each of these men and women were constant to their role as mortals. They had lived not only through the tough times of a great depression, but world war as well. What attitudes did they embody to give them hope during times of rationing food and military service? How did they sleep at night with the fear they might be rearing children alone? Clearly without perfection they sought to live with dignity, a testament to the grace and determination rooted at their core.

One such elder, I called Thomas; he was Tom to the other residents that lived where I cooked. Always positive, a jokester with a kind heart, he overlooked the fussiness (if not utter sense of self orientation) of the women with whom he shared a table at mealtime. His death seemed more sudden, as an interruption to a bite of his adored over-easy eggs. Why was his outlook on life upbeat and positive when others' expressions were prone to pessimism, a half empty state? Had he suffered any more or less than the others? I wonder what effect his death will ultimately have on the attitudes of the females he left behind at the "difficult" table.

"Maturing is not just about aging. It's about taking responsibility for the space you occupy," Maya Angelou affirms. With the bounds and limits of expanding ourselves, we as conscious individuals attempt --and often fail-- to express our soul's aspirations, the potential for which we are born. Ego driven, we are afraid to look, act or BE older. We neglect putting aside some of our self absorption to consider others. Media reports to us ad nauseam the countless ways to remain ageless and carefree. Have we forgotten we are more than these bodies? Are we so obsessed with how we appear to others that we neglect taking stock of how we might give to others? Are we then misusing the space we occupy?

Aging might be about uncovering some mystery of our larger story. Some might call life fated, predetermined. Others think it's nothing more than a random roll of the dice. Matthew Sanford, paralyzed in a car accident at the age of thirteen, wonders in his book, *Waking: A Memoir of Trauma and Transcendence,* if his suffering gave him two lives. He questioned if "life has been a preparation for itself." While enduring indescribable pain during recovery --screws drilled into his skull, body casts painfully applied and worn for months, severe organ damage that precluded eating-- he witnessed a curious connection between his waking mind and broken body.

Needing to undergo a second body cast and knowing the shock the first one caused, his mother quietly issued a desperate suggestion: "try leaving your body for a while." While surprised by his mother's plea, he understood its meaning. Having been forced to sustain such brutal pain since the accident, he learned he could leave his body to survive. He could relocate his consciousness to avoid physical suffering. He could observe himself with his mind.

During the months and years of recovery that did not include walking again, Sanford employed that state of silent observation. This practice became his daily routine, one that initially offered him reprieve from the profound violence his body endured. Ultimately, he discovered that quiet state offered him access to his body when he practiced yoga. Today he employs his fate to impact the lives of others through sharing his experience of the body-mind relationship. His healing stories have illustrated his search, not for answers, but as an appreciation and belief in the experience.

What is our practice, our consciousness? UC Berkeley's philosophy professor and Institute of Cognitive and Brain Sciences member, Alva Noe, in *Out of Our Heads*, states, it's "something we do actively, in the dynamic interaction of the world around us." Could this interaction be our personal way of moving through the moments of a maturing life? Are we open to the possibilities we are capable of, without being stuck in negative, one-way thinking that undermines the potential of who we are and what we can offer those around us? Some spiritual traditions advocate "taking your life on the path." Without avoiding the pain and tragedy that occurs in our lives, can we use it as a platform for change, for maintaining awareness, and moving toward wisdom?

I recently shared a Thanksgiving table with my youngest son and three of his friends. During our lively dinner conversation around a bountiful table, I asked these 20-somethings how emotional incidents in their lives had informed them about their future. They didn't dodge the question; they invited it into their awareness and our dialogue. Their shared events ranged from being paralyzed for 18 hours to witnessing the ravages of poverty and infectious disease in a foreign country.

All these privileged and bright young people shared a common reply about their future. They wanted to affect some kind of change. Whether through charitable, political, environmental or humanitarian effort, these "kids" were choosing an attitude of optimism and hope. Idealistic? Yes. Possible? Why not? Robert Kennedy believed "Each time a man stands up for an ideal, or acts to improve the lot of others, or strikes out against injustice, he sends forth a tiny ripple of hope…"

"The best way out is through." Robert Frost's words ring true when considering how to traverse the interval between life and death. Every experience informs. Every question matters. How we react along the way is a reflection of how far we've come in seeking the truth and understanding who we are at our best.

Last summer Richard handed me a paper napkin for the homemade bread Kathy had just pulled from the oven. Printed on the face-up side was some wisecrack about bringing a hot dish, but NOT green bean casserole. On the back, he'd jotted the Viking Nine Noble Virtues. The second one was truth. "Truth in the sense of honesty, as essential to personal honor" my Google-pedia informed me. The Viking laws held an honor code which maintained that extreme honesty with oneself as well as with others was key in respecting this principal of truth.

Whose truth is true? Is there only one reality? Our compass in forging through the joys and trials on our path is uniquely individual. Perhaps this journey requires ample amounts of Viking Noble Virtue number one: Courage. Can we court the possibility of a way through whatever comes next, by not only daring to ask and wonder, but by being willing to seek and open ourselves enough to find? If a prudent question is one half of wisdom, then surely we're well on our way! Woody Allen may have been onto something when he remarked, "Seventy percent of success in life is showing up." What does the remaining thirty percent look like to you? Have you truly finished changing? Or are you just finished?

"Nature often holds up a mirror so we can see more clearly the ongoing processes of growth, renewal, and transformation of our lives."

- Mary Ann Brussat

rEvolution

Spring's ripening in the Pacific Northwest rivals the burgeoning pregnancy of a new mother. Full, sensual, and flushed with color, its many buds swell with the onset of a new season. While on my walk today, I noticed the beginnings of fuchsia-pink rhododendrons, a variegation of hues tinting hellebore, and the spidery tentacles of golden witchhazel. Their splendor planted me as close to drunkenness as I could possibly have been without alcohol touching my lips! Spring is my favorite time of year. It promises and celebrates potential. In the case of perennial growth, the old flora has let go its final hold on life and the tender, young foliage literally spirals forth. Nature in her resplendent cycle of change reminds me that it is the liberation of the outworn that opens a space for something brand new to develop, to progress.

In 1923 Czechoslovakia, a special communion service was introduced where the need for a symbolic ritual would bind people more closely together, rather than alienating them within their different religious traditions. Literally, a flower communion practice blossomed. This was a simple service in which people were asked to bring a flower of their choice and place it in a communal bouquet. The idea symbolized that no two blossoms, as well as no two individuals, were exactly identical. By exchanging flowers, each person recognized he or she possessed their own unique contribution toward a shared community and the willingness to disregard what might divide.

Much like the natural world, we humans have, in a lifetime, the opportunity to give birth to ourselves time and again, if we choose. We do this through career change, new relationships, geographic relocation, intellectual or artistic curiosity, social change, education, and an open mind. In a word: growth. We come full circle from an older experience, perhaps a dying one, converting the withered has-been to the vibrant what-will-be.

In the last year and a half my daughter has returned to an academic environment. This endeavor has been no easy task considering a ten year gap between educational objectives, an energetic family with four children --one nearly brand new-- and perhaps a preliminary notion of trepidation. The strength of character, however, that Hana possesses is boundless. This was evident when she was a little girl. She pushed the edges, sometimes gently while other times seemed more like free-falling from the high dive. As any child development professional will tell you: that is her job.

The bottom line is evolution. As in our natural world where nothing is static, so it is with humans. We keep on keeping on. Through a diligent desire to question what can be, we shed our outdated thoughts and actions. We raise the bar. It is imperative that we do so. My 30-something daughter will graduate this spring. Her hard-working efforts will benefit not only herself, but her family who have witnessed her determined example, and the many people she will serve as a health professional.

Collectively, transforming the old to the new can bring about great change in humanity. Simple endeavors such as kindness, generosity, respect, tolerance and advocacy are a few means of seeding this cycle of growth. The actions of "raising awareness, creating impact and transforming the heart," according to Nipun Mehta in *Daily Good News That Inspires*, are as vital as the evolutionary process of winter-to-spring. Nature reflects to us our interconnectedness, the One we all are part of.

Could death --letting the old fall away-- be the single best agent of change? Can we as humans be inspired by nature's model of metamorphosis? Can we unearth our part in this process? Shall we elevate the principles of being in the world from greed to giving, indifference to compassion, and stagnation to revolution? As nature proclaims every spring when delicate shoots and buds appear, the fruition of life is essential. It is our earnest, individual, responsibility --perhaps our gift-- to persistently rekindle that spirit of positive growth and renewal. Borrowing poet Mary Oliver's brilliant question, I ask you: "What is it you plan to do with your wild and precious life?"

"Under any circumstance, always do your best, no more and no less."

- Don Miguel Ruiz, *The Four Agreements*

AfterWords

On any given day in most of our cities, there are a multitude of cultural activities to delight. What good fortune for those of us who can count on the inspiration from these creative experiences we have the opportunity to partake. John Frame, sculptor-turned-stop-action-animator claims his new work isn't expressionist, conceptual, or even craft, but rather a blend led purely by his intuition. His current exhibit at the Portland Art Museum is ingenious. The story he tells portrayed through his new world art is hypnotic, mysterious and even a bit disturbing. Frame admits his work is representative of not only his intuition but by also asking the age-old questions: "Who am I? What am I doing here?" He says his new film-making, non-narrative, non-linear art came to him in a 12-hour hypnopompic state --time between dream and wakening.

On another floor of the museum is Russian-American painter Mark Rothko's, exhibit. Equally as magnificent and thought provoking, Rothko's work spans the surreal to color field painting. His later art meant to evoke the big emotions --tragedy, ecstasy, doom, and a sense of spirituality-- are dynamic in both stature and hue. When I visited this exhibit at P.A.M. on a rainy Saturday afternoon, I was fascinated by a man standing daringly close to one tall orange, red, and yellow painting. The watchful volunteers in the room had their eye on the museum-goer for different reasons than I did. I was struck by the fact he was dressed in the very same colors as the painting. What emotions or thought processes were evoked in this human so completely taken with Rothko's artwork, his nose nearly touched its surface?

"Uncertainty is intrinsic to the process of finding out what you don't know, not a weakness to avoid." Neil Gershenfeld, director of Massachusetts Institute of Technology's Centre for Bits and Atoms, made this statement as part of his reflection and reply to "What scientific concept would improve everybody's cognitive toolkit?" "We must learn to love uncertainty..." writes Alok Jha, UK's *Guardian* correspondent for this report. Could not knowing, and the act of seeking, be a bridge spanning something in us as thinking humans? Is this uncertainty and wanting-to-know scientific in nature, merely a brain function? How do we comprehend the world?

Adam Frank writes in Science as *Spiritual Practice,* intuition is a prerequisite for knowing how to pose a question. He understands that gut-level feeling is about paying attention to the world as it presents itself in the countless ways life unfolds. His belief that what merges science and authentic spiritual endeavor isn't the nature of a truth each might claim, but an "ethic and practice of inquiry itself."

AfterWords

In celebration of my 60th birthday recently, Julie gifted me with a small satin bag filled with various words imprinted on tiny cards. Tolerant. Thoughtful. Forgiving. Heroic. Amorous. Though not a complete lexis, the collection of 33 positive human qualities are muse worthy of a daily draw. I consider the pick of the day as I go about my routine or activities. Somehow the word mirrors something to me during those hours. Often the word evokes a memory, a hope and on tough days, a sadness. Occasionally, I have a vivid image of someone or a place that holds importance to me. Words have the power to make me think, and whether I'm engaging my "cognitive toolkit" or the deepest place of my soul, I respond. The best way I know how, right now.

Today the sun struggles to dispel the morning's chill. The din of traffic does not diminish the birds' song. However numb the toes and visible the breath, scent of evergreen and smiles on passing faces, illuminate the day in one of Portland's city parks. I walk the man-made pathways, sturdy, city maintained and easily followed. Other trails, earthy and muddy, cause my feet to slip requiring necessity of balance. My mind is silent. It is not. Life is a dichotomy, treading one moment the smooth route and the next, muddled and circuitous. What is your word for the day? What are your questions? How will you give nothing more or less than your best, each step of the way?

"And the day came when the risk to remain tight in a bud was more painful than the risk it took to blossom."

- Anais Nin

Colophon

Text set in Minion Pro
Titles Myrad Pro
Designed in Adobe Indesign
Printed in the USA

You may reach the author through her
blog:

http://pamelaiwright.org/author/

info@onespiritpress.com
www.onespiritpress.com